RUNNING NEAR THE END OF THE WORLD

. . . .

Winner of the

Edwin Ford Piper

Poetry Award

Publication of this book

was made possible with

the generous assistance of

Janet Piper

RUNNING
NEAR
THE END
OF THE
WORLD

. . . .

POEMS BY WALTER PAVLICH

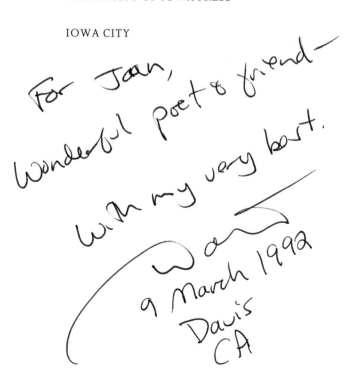

UNIVERSITY OF IOWA PRESS

IOWA CITY

For Joan,
Wonderful poet & friend —
With my very best.

Wa—
9 March 1992
Davis
CA

University of Iowa Press,
Iowa City 52242
Copyright © 1992
by Walter Pavlich
All rights reserved
Printed in the
United States of America
First edition, 1992

Design by Richard Hendel

Printed on acid-free paper

Library of Congress Cataloging-in-
Publication Data

Pavlich, Walter, 1955–
    Running near the end of the world:
    poems/by Walter Pavlich.—1st ed.
        p.   cm.
    ISBN 0-87745-358-6 (acid-free paper)
    I. Title.
PS3566.A88R8   1992   91-31623
811'.54—dc20   CIP

for Sandy

for my family

Joy all over me . . .

The world didn't give it to me,

and the world can't take it.

The world can't take

this joy I've got.

—Willie Neal Johnson

Some of these poems appeared in the following publications.

Anemone: "The Final Trout"; Calapooya Collage: "Saying Good-bye to the Wolf Eels," "Before the Last Checkpoint, Leaving Prison, after Teaching My Class"; Chariton Review: "Fire Crew, 1910"; Cincinnati Poetry Review: "Looking at Buster Keaton," "Buster Keaton during the Shooting of a Low-Budget Mexican Movie, 1934"; Commonweal: "Flying to the Fire with the Doors Off," "Hardhat Pillow," "The Hand Beginning to Burn"; Fine Madness: "Among the Tidemarks," "Fog"; High Plains Literary Review: "A Theory of Birds"; Laurel Review: "Buster Keaton Sees His First Movie," "Buster Keaton and Fatty Arbuckle in California, 1917"; Mānoa: "Killing the Man Who Wanted to Die," "Oliver Hardy near the End," "Overlooking the Pacific, Family Reunion, Celebrating My Brother's Child, Ecola State Park," "Stan Laurel, Retired, at His Oceana Apartment, 1962," "On the Life and Death of Stan Laurel's Son," "Oliver Hardy, a Little Tired," "In the Belly of the Ewe," "Cloud Street"; Nebraska Review: "Last Picture"; Northwest Review: "Lost Comedy," "Stan's"; Poetry: "Running near the End of the World," © 1991 by the Modern Poetry Association; Poetry Flash: "Before the Last Checkpoint, Leaving Prison, after Teaching My Class"; Raccoon: "Three Hearts of the Octopus"; Seattle Review: "The Eel and the Man with One Arm," "This Blue, These Floating Things"; Shenandoah: "Visiting Day," "After an Afternoon Showing of Laurel & Hardy's Brats"; Visions: "Late August Isolations"; Willamette Week: "The Deaf and the Blind."

Several of these poems also appeared in the chapbooks Of Things Odd and Therefore Beautiful, Leaping Mountain Press, 1987; Theories of Birds and Water, Owl Creek Press, 1990; and The Lost Comedy, Howlet Press, 1991.

Certain poems were reprinted in the following anthologies: "Fog" in Floating Island IV, Floating Island Publications, 1989; "Hardhat Pillow" and "Flying to the Fire with the Doors Off" in Labor in the Post-

Industrial Age, Pig Iron Press, 1990; "Lost Comedy" in *The Decade Dance*, Sandhills Press, 1991; and "My Father and I Try on Masks of Laurel and Hardy" in *Movieworks*, Little Theatre Press, 1990.

"On the Life and Death of Stan Laurel's Son" also appeared in *Pushcart Prize XV*, 1990.

My thanks to William Heyen, Leonard Nathan, Lucien Stryk, and others for friendships I can feel.

I'd also like to thank certain gospel singers: the Reverend Claude Jeter, the Reverend Julius Cheeks, Willie Banks, the Spirit of Memphis Quartet, and especially Willie Neal Johnson and the Gospel Keynotes, who help me to carry on.

CONTENTS

. . . .

I I I

PART I

. . . .

And so he told us how he had been sewn
into the belly of a ewe by his father
and a couple of uncles, because his legs
would not unfold after delivery,

as though in the womb the ligaments
had looped around bone and kinked,
heels clamped to thighs, a spiritual
cramp from God, an execration

for what they did not know.
His mother kept next to him in the barn,
pinching off sheep ticks, not sleeping
while the baby slept, helping the animal

to its side when its own legs hardened
from the standing, and kept the hooves
from kicking his exposed tottering head.
On the second Sunday of his life

they slit him free, limbs in a dangle
like severed rubberbands, and slaughtered
the beast with the same knife for that
day's blessed supper. He told us this

in the yard of the world's largest prison,
on the way back to his cell where
he continued to cough up little wet
moths of blood, where he was always

cold, always ashamed, as he gathered
the wool blanket up and around him.

. . . .

We were ordinary anywhere but there.

Hands on cast iron. Mono-
syllabics of lifting, the body
in a sequence of tissue jacks
and blood hydraulics.

Forehead venous. A grunt helped
with the first few inches.
Strain-stragglers of red and black
larvae squirmed in each eye.

My father told me I had
deltoids, lats, pecs. When
I worked out hard my triceps
hummed. White limestone

for grip, to pacify the calluses,
a belt to keep the back
from detaching or intestines
blurting like a dropped sack

of grume-filled balloons,
during squats, clean-
and-jerks, dead lifts,
inclines, chins, dips,

and curls. We ended
each time watching our arms
in the mirror. He stored
his in his workshirt.

We were ordinary
anywhere but there. Dungeon,
submarine, cellar. In the wet-
ash rainlight. In the one

lightbulb we unscrewed and
carried to the socket we needed.
Barbells paralyzed until
we hoisted their silence

as high as we could,
hosannas of unholy sweat.
No one ever took them.
We knew how to lift them down.

Above lodgepole, ponderosa,
tamarack, a sharp drunk globe out
of balance, the world backspinning,
under and behind us. I'm listening
for the treetops scratching
our ship's belly, the pilot
with folded beer cans behind his seat,
and you leaning out, shouting, as we tap
into an updraft just before the next ridge.

We are lightning's employees,
mountain-scrapers, twice the water
in our canteens that we piss out.
You are upslope in the smoke,
sparks spitting on you, where you shouldn't
be, daring the fire to step over
your gashed line. I am
where it started, calling
calling. The flames flaring up
the underside of your name.

THE TALLEST MAN IN THE FOREST
Camel's Hump Lookout, Lolo National Forest, Montana

. . . .

Up in the hawks
where they float all afternoon,
above beargrass, fireweed,
huckleberry, paintbrush,
you live inside the storms,
counting lightning, overtime,
other mathematics of fire.

You azimuth and guess
smokes from waterdogs,
radio the sirens on.
You've sent me to southern
exposures where the sun
first tows the fire
out of the ground.

                    Saw-flash
or a hand-sized mirror
sends some signal-light
back to you, "Fine. Sweating.
Lasso a cloud, like a vaporous
blimp, rupture it over here."

You drip hot sauce
into your coffee, night-
juice for the cumulo-
nimbus idling over Idaho.

8

It'll send me chasing
sparks. It'll sit you
in the chair boosted
by insulators, little shot
glasses, your dog on
your lap throwing up
the jackrabbit she chased into
her belly that morning.

You count toward each thunder
after the lightning sharpens
around you.

Not so silly now, the grouse
(fool hens) who watched as you
stoned their throats.
You sit, the tallest man
in the forest, as the nails
begin to hum and glow,
some of them spitting
clean out of the walls.

Note: *Waterdogs are small, low morning clouds that resemble smoke.*

. . . .

We admire its electric grace,
limbless undulations
enforced by the right angles
of watercolor glass,
water temperature like the last
few minutes of a bath.
It has all but given up
its eyes, and alone
is able to stun only itself.

A man wanders away
from his family, a shirtsleeve
tucked and pinned inside
his vest like a hollow excuse.
You say: a poverty of shoulder,
your hand wilting into mine.

I remember a childhood friend
who at birth was the breathing
half of Siamese twins.
They had dissected
him from his blue other,
from an arm and leg
they had once both owned.

In the next tank
cowfish blow lewd
yellow kisses at anyone.
But the man and the eel
have become their own display.

He's found a temporary arm
meandering lost before him
with enough voltage
in the slow and lonely S's
of its murky interior
to flutter his heart.

This eel is not an eel.
It's just a fish executing
the water around it.

Damp shares of cloud
slide overhead. We wonder
about the tingler
that runs the phantom gamut
of where his arm was
on the way to give
his wife a hug,
a half a hug.

He is a lesson
in equilibrium,
our souvenir of poise
in an afternoon
of roundabout tellings:
ex-lovers and losing.
How it takes most our lives
of embracing too many others
to get ourselves closer to right.

. . . .

He chooses Stan, conforms his head
to the mask's cave, focusing to find
the eyeholes, like binoculars handed over
from someone else. His nose rests
in the thin latex approximation of a proboscis,
his chin unsupported in the comic's long jaw.
He's doubled himself, must do the thinking
for both. Here is a serious man
in the vacant skull of a genius.

Becoming Ollie doesn't hurt. No scrape
of his face over mine. I can wear him
backwards, or sideways and talk
through one stiff, useless ear.
I've been planning for the belly, but the charm's
a problem, and I want to scold:

"Stop yelling so much at your wife,"
and
"Why don't you hold her more often?"

We're drinking beer through our eyes;
the lips don't work.
There were no words in the heads
when I bought them. This pantomime's
unfunny to anyone but us.

Too hot to laugh inside them
much longer, we breathe in
our breath's hot clear fog
close as a summer attic.
Time to be father and son again,
slapstick, gaffes and gags endlessly
rehearsed, ready to pass on the act
to any like-men who need one.

. . . .

He cannot hear my fingers'
soft braille reading
hallway air to the bathroom,
inching along the gallery
of foreheads and cheeks,
lips and noses of the pictures
that outlived the faces
they tried to be.

I might as well be blind
on a corner at dusk
planning ways to sleepwalk
a path through traffic.

My sudden light
injures his dozing.
He coughs across his pillow
bursts of red lightning.

I have been out
late spending his money.
We are both out
of work and privately
worry about one another.

In the index of his dreams,
did I interrupt a peacock
yowing in the zoo after closing,
tinfoil scraping over
a sandlot outfield?

He reaches for his hearing aid,
which when aroused
sings like a toy bird
from its copper heart,
and hooks it behind his ear
to the worn spot,
banana-shaped,
where the follicles have been smothered.
It sifts the dialects
of a wrong number
from cat's heat,
a refrigerator
from houseflies waking.

"Walter," he tries at me,
like shooting baskets
in the dark,
and I pretend I don't
hear him.

We've adopted each other
as strangers we might
not want to know.
We've rehearsed our lives
for many quick farewells.

For now it's back
to the bed that absorbs me
with a common moan,
back down the alley
along the rectangles
of glass and wood,
groping toward morning
over the years reproduced
in the trances of black and white.

· ·

On the beach where the boy with lavender
hair washed up cold as his wetsuit,

where on another occasion two young Amish
women in wispy pastels (as though seeing the unseeable)
flirted with the surf,
God's cold hand on the soft meat
behind their knees,

where a dog once gnashed my shin,
teeth drilling with silver like
fountain pen nibs into the skin

(I ladled hand-cup after cup of
brine-purger, imagining the weekly
stomach shots, needle the size of
a partially telescoped car antenna),

someone had lashed a driftwood cross
and twined to it a doll, headless,
seawater down the o of her neck,

but just who had splashed
a sloppy vest of paint, ill-fitting blue,
Easter blueness, on the gull
begging amongst beggars,
a mock consecration of color

so that one could patch the sky
with it, or complete a bastard trinity—

day-blue lavender boy,
plaything crucifix resurrected by the next tide.

BEFORE THE LAST CHECKPOINT, LEAVING PRISON, AFTER TEACHING MY CLASS

. . . .

How would I have explained
a bird under my shirt
(nestling born under a rifle,
fallen from its aerie under
the tower) to the guard
who studies me with his hands.
He won't find a leather-
punch rose, or heart
earrings shaped from teeth.
I am an import on the way
out with this to declare:

I think the bird's yellow
mouth linings are really lips
and because of its aphasia
it cries "keep keep keep."
I think each man here
has a third wing that
confounds the other two
so that there is no way up
and the sky is only
a color to have come from.

. . . .

Most fathers knew more words
than mine. "Yesterday I whent
to see Ruby at the nursing home."
Or, "Poor old Pete; another goner."
My mother memorized lists
from a neighbor's *Reader's Digest*.
I can hear her down the hallway
from her heavy summer bedroom:
ignominy, inveracity, irrevocable.

An inmate I see Saturday mornings
wants me to read
the Constitution. The dictionary
has all the apparatus he needed.
Wooden boat, not metal, won't echo,
gas station rags wrapped
around the oarlock moan,
chain-lengths intimate,
snug to bulge her haunch bones,
where he used to love to kiss.
Deflate the intestines,
jab out all the gas.
Dip her in.

His children only know
the alphabets of their names.
One can almost make a lake
out of Katy.

I help him write his letters home.
"Daddy loves. Daddy misses."

In pink that hurts,
left-out-butter dresses,
spinach shoes, in colors
of some lewd Easter,
they meet their men
in a tennis court
with a cyclone roof
and gash-wire. Children
darken from truck-tire games,
little running smudges.
This is touch time,
from toe nuzzling
to magnets in the hips
down the arm along
the shoulder to an easy-going hand
shading a breast.
A seal, a double shade
without any wrinkles of light.
Sometimes girlfriends and wives
at the same time.
Sucking on an earring.
Licking some flamingo
lipstick off the sharp
opening of a root beer car
after they've gone.

The whole train leaning up
against the engine, the Starlighter's
wheels cutting sparks into thistles,
men in the swaying urinals
pressed into mirrors,
bingo tokens on the club car floor,
a grandmother's tipped vodka meandering
through cards' sticky solitaire. Now he's
dead as the lunch soaking
in your belly's afternoon.

His head drops one way,
button off an excitable shirt,
the popped sack of his body
shines red and new
over downtown streets,
fresh glaze on the puckered tar.

A leg's kicked free,
mannequin in the ditch,
nude as a popsicle stick,
rugged circle of a bottlecap
quarter-screwed on his thigh.

He felt his brain floating
in a vinegar sea.
So the tracks became a bed,
the train the dream,
gravel plush as he imagined.

And everything on the 12:05
became an inventory to assist him:

the bottom lip of an often-used mouth
kissed on a squeezed paper cup,
plastic thimbles of turning half & half,
slabs of soap palmed, brittle,
a heavy collection of sighs and irritations . . .

A blush of summer light
was the last quiet thing
on his face. Were there new colors
and worries, he wondered,
as he thought he felt soft weather,
as everything for a moment gathered over him
to kill him again & again & again.

. . . .

He chose more of forever,
summer when it tumbles down.
Empty white snail shells unwind.
Ice-plants rust and crumble
underfoot, their roots clinching
the loose grip of the sand.

One more season without touching
the deer's blood-warm nervous ear.
A cough follows it
into the dunes.
    The horizon
a pause he can rest at.
He tries to name the three miles
of natural dazzle in between.

Trouble with colors—they fall
apart before he can say them,
fade or bruise on their way
to his lips: methyl blue,

mallard, glass green. They repeat
in the wings and well-rubbed
head of a capsized fly.
It had walked a transparence,
a drifting clearness, until
the sun overfilled it,

baked it in its own black,
near the dead temperature
of a tearose moth, and the sticky
unattached cloud of a web,
grounded, torn and smoky.

He calls it blurred tin.

. . . .

So one man writes *A Field Guide*
to the Atmosphere, and another
steals a copy from the prison library
along with *Handbook for Painting*
Skies.
      Thief of katabatic winds
and sunrise white, undersun,
varve, appendix of twilight phenomena,
the chapter on disguising dusk.

When he looks through his window
there is color and reason for everything.

The hail is not the shit they must
walk through on the way
to a dark dinner, but graupel

color of a stepped-on wedding dress.

On the way back he might remember
"most objects are seen because of
light from some other luminous body"

so does not see the men ahead
in laminar flow,
or their hand-fires of cigarettes,

and the coughs and breaths behind him
do not register on his Beaufort Numbers
for Wind Force.

Instead he walks alone on cloud street
back into his cell, through
the stellars, the needles, the ice crystals,

the halo of his yet-to-be brushed-in moon.

PART II

A five-cent flicker
in a nickelodeon where a pharmacy
used to be. A few little
broken moons of aspirin under
the folding pine seats. Suits
and squeaking. Match flare
and much smoking.

              Keaton
stands in the back, his whole
face balanced on a thought.
On the screen (a bedsheet tautly
tacked) ocean waves lurping
toward the front row.
Some wonder if they'll get
wet.
      Water out of a wall.
No water. But water
funneled through a visible
tube of light. Buster puts
his hand on the hot machine.
Buzz of gears resonates
up his arm. Delicious hum.

He steps between projector
and sheet—a girl almost
drowning on his hand.

. . . .

Evidently a face.
Like a thumbnail with one
expression, with eyes that don't
go through a person but go
in and stay there, feeling
their way unobtrusively around
a sadness, or, recognizing pain,
glancing it like two ants
interrupted by each other.

It is the face of a clock
with its hands in its ears.
And its time is the beginning
and end of any flower.

Temperature of such a face:
tapwater over a dead wrist;
or someone's hair just before
they awaken after a long sleep.

You would not know where
to kiss this face
unless you married it

and even then sometimes
it seemed like human glass

so your lips would only
be a pink stupefaction,
something for a handkerchief

to make fun out of.

It is a face bouncing
a joyless ball
down the backstreets of innocence.

It is the face on the ball too.

AFTER AN AFTERNOON SHOWING OF
LAUREL & HARDY'S *BRATS*

· ·

They play themselves as children,
that is, sons & fathers,

so on the split-screen, quadrupled bother.
The boys irk & puzzle & fluster the men,

Ollie stifling annoyance, provoked further by Stan.
But it's a matinee of bosh, or would you rather

plunk a vase on the skull of the love who matters?
They're a family of four, four thumbs on one hand,

a skylarking, a tussling, a pitiful band.
Yet when the pic's over, lights on, there're colors,

we smile all night at our black-and-white others—
whelps and bantlings overcrowding a thirty-foot screen.

. . . .

hungover, droozy, vertiginous.
A full morning shooting rigamarole
on a wooden I-beam. Oliver trips off
(loose shoelace), fractures a sugar pine platform,
the safety net springing him up
into the atmosphere he yelled through.

Stan bleaches, his makeup sweating.
Two hundred feet to Los Angeles
below. He leaps to the hook
of a block and tackle, swings out
beyond the camera's stretch,
dangling above the car horns,
midway between nothing
and concrete stardom.

At least that's what he thinks
as he's reeled back in and scolded.
By afternoon he's improvised it
into the script. Again and again
he sways over the city,
snagged by the collar,
legs pedaling an invisible bicycle.
From the next short on there'll be
a stunt-double, one he'll teach
to hurt like him. And all of the laughs
will be secured, earned closer
to the sober ground.

· ·

Some days
mostly liquid gags,
splashed and dapper
with spritz through a candlestick phone,
bathtub backfall,
a dive into the lily fountain,
goldfish in trouser cuffs,
some pond left over
in his derby.

Monday's not healed.
This foolery hurts worse
on Tuesday. On Wednesday
he'll be asked to swallow
a waterfall.

With his spitcurl tassels
combed back over his head,
he's Babe again,
a heated robe, coffee,
a cold lamb lunch
oiled with wine,
its thyme mustard lingers
in the mustache growing up
into his nostrils.

For the seventh time he strolls
off a curb . . .
unable to walk on the puddle
taller than he is.

Where the Hollywood snowball
(cornstarch, mashed potatoes
and cold cream) fastens long
enough on his brow for the zooming
ring to twist tight
for the dolorous close-up,
a real tear sac breaks,
and his iris bruises
in black and white.

. . . .

Buster no longer had to follow
acts like Don the Talking Dog or
the Three Shrinking Sisters of Sashay.

Fatty was teaching him what
the camera could see. On film
they didn't have to use a cardboard
cow. Midnight could be followed by
a lemon rising.

One could backflip off
a castle and land in a pail
of molasses.

       A mustache
was usually meaner.

Series of moths a lover's stutter.

Words were cement drying
to the plot, and verbs
shoes stuck in it.

It was all in the doing.

Like neighbors watching neighbors
mouth an argument through
closed bedroom windows.

Like making a mute brick laugh.

. . . .

If the scene calls
for surprise

pretend the last
chocolate in the box

is hollow
and you eat into

a bee. Then
blink

like brassy wings.
The exag-

gerators chew
wasps

or put a hornet
in their watch-

pocket. Don't
be a smart

Alexander.
Remember rump

humor. Use
your silly buttocks.

Ease down
on a rubber

nail. Taste
your bee.

. . . .

Innocence combs Stan's hair
straight up. Drizzle limps it.
Cameras and lights mire.
Sand in everything,
film cans' grit, grainy sandwiches,
in the pancake makeup
peppered into their faces.

In love with a mermaid,
Oliver waggles his tie,
waiting. The tide's out.
Stan pulls on a garden hose,
walks it out to where
the surf was. He's filling
in the tide, so Oliver
can see his sweetheart again.

Hours later, the ocean's back.
No girl with the sea
in her. A driftlog's rolled
over sleeping Oliver.
Thin for the first time.
The last, after the strokes,
the plot of his coma unscripted.
Stan puts his cardboard pal
under his arm. The two-reeler
flutters a goodbye.

This is the lost comedy.
If one is two, then one half
isn't enough. Stan won't
perform without him.
Maybe a soft-shoe
now and then in the kitchen,
in his slippers before dinner,
when they both would've quit
for the day.

BUSTER KEATON DURING THE SHOOTING OF A
LOW-BUDGET MEXICAN MOVIE, 1934

. . . .

Whiskey for breakfast.
                    It takes
a hot chrome elevator
down his throat.
                    Last night?
There must have been one.
Creepy haze of an underlit
cantina. And kissing the faces
off the stone frogs in the fountain.

Nerves like plastic bone
wind chimes before a storm.

Frenzy of clacks.

Pie gag day. Blackberry
smeared on the wigged blonde.
Lemon-meringue for the brunette.

For Señor Buster more
whiskey. A warm beer
for lunch. When he coughs
he feels cacti in his lungs.

But he's working. And this
morning only a little blood
from the anus.

For nine days, two Stanleys, one funny,
one drowning, brain capsizing in its own blood,
lungs miscarrying air
from one breath to the next, a tenant
shut in its dissembling body,
incubator too much like a show room.

Stan's tired of crying on screen.
Off, that's all he can do. The night nurse
steals his exhausted handkerchief, hides it
under her sleeve on her wrist pulse.
Someday these tears might be worth something.

Stan Jr. dies without one chuckle
to smooth out his face, and is burned
into a little pile his father
pretends he keeps in a clear candy jar.
Every morning for luck Stan rubs
a fingerprint on the glass

cold as a spoon, his son
neutral inside. Then off to the laughter
works where he invents the same smile
each day, and that way of walking,
as if the ground were a ledge, and he's strolling
alone, three steps off the earth.

. . . .

Too abdominous to belong in your bed?
Afraid I might trouble
your icebox? I practiced until
I had butterflies in my heels,
laid down some floaty steps.

Little applause in a mirror.
Humid drapes of me.
OK, I've had steak and pie
for breakfast. I can still fail
funnier than you.

You want a monster
in the fat.
Mushrooms of butter in my blood.

The French laugh in French.
British sneeze the North Sea.
They want to touch us.
On the oceanliner over a woman
clutched greedy between my hams.

Children don't know me
at the market. They point
and hide behind the lettuce.
A gorbellied man shopping
alone. Beef and ale.
New little potatoes,
their brush-scrubbed faces
I'll slice neatly in two.

LAST PICTURE

Laurel and Hardy on location near Cannes, 1950,
making Utopia, a.k.a. Atoll K a.k.a. Robinson Crusoeland

. . . .

Stan sits in a tin trailer
between takes, sweat and budget
makeup curdle into sloppy wens.
He requests one of the fans
used to fake a typhoon.
The rain-machine's water
addles, a dirty-nail-in-the-mouth taste.
And it must rain all day
on both of them.

He practices his scene
with the brummagem lobster,
vinyl prop he'll burp and baby.
A stagehand tried to dye it red
but Stan didn't want his pet
to have a cooked look, even
though the picture's not in color.
He's worried the wires will show,
that its scuttle might shoot
more like a scamper or a trot.

Mustn't let the director
(who swears at him in Italian)
find out that Stan's prostate's solid,
his urine like a rope
on fire with an occasional knot.
And Oliver's at his heaviest,

over 350, somersaults
of his heart breaking veins.

It's taken all these months
to make an uncopyrighted fizzle.
Such promise too: they inherit
a sailboat, Ollie's the admiral,
Stan's the crew. Then an island
pops up out of the sea.
Just the two of them
spilling bouillabaisse on
each other, sleeping in the same
hammock, throwing each other
the lifesaver that hesitates,
then drops like a finished career
to the bottom of the sea.

· ·

He's misplaced his wife's
name. She carries the bath
to him. Washes everyplace
he's famous first.

His mind on dissolve.
He cannot say Stan.
He cannot say
a thing. Not help,
not comb, not summer.

Aguish white gravy.
Puddles of it. Baking-
soda biscuits mulled
and put back.
Crumbs down the chest
of his nightshirt.
Suspenders won't hold
him up. Now weighs less
than he lost.

Honey (she prunes his mustache)
you and Stan are on the tv tonight.

Cocoa on his chin.
The blue of black and white.
A comedian in each eye.
Funny fellows he'd someday
like to meet.

. . . .

Behind him the smaze of Santa Monica;
oceanward, pelicans release from their cruising,
disengage from the same height as his balcony

to fish from thirty feet of May.
Colliding with a swell's no accident,
appearing awkward perfectly,

escalading without a headache,
fish roaming the translucent receding sea of its pouch.
Grace is the stunt bungled precisely.

To blunder his rump exactly
against the counterfeit buzz saw,
to drop his face on the nave

of a wedding cake, groom and bride
divorced by his forehead.
He walks over the bridge of the audience's

laughter to the next drubbing. Rubber bricks
konking him to the peal of a propman
ascending the stairs of a xylophone.

When the silents ended he thought
his lisp would curse him,
weaken the sinlessness of "Stanley."

His speech did not defame him
and Oliver could sing tenor-sweet.
When they fought on film

they knew the volleys of arguments
were manufactured in silence,
that words came later.

With their tiffs, the broom handle in the eye
was the beginning of forgetting,
forgiving each other the way to more disaster.

PART III

. . . .

Dusk.
Helicopter landing in a field
of rabbits. A fire shoos
itself under the vision
of the hill
and up. I hear others
wondering from far away
"What do you think he's doing
on his birthday?"

Well, star candles are just
now being lit, and orange stump
and sour pine candles deepen as
I recede only to become
a headlamp poking my way
through the dark. I dig
into this cake of earth,
duff, fur, cones.
The wind switches, feeling
its way downslope, haze
a smoky bedspread over the field,
where a hundred gifts were hiding—
the scattering majesty of fire and rabbits.

· ·

We collapse the horses
to their knees in the creek,
hide them under the soaked
blankets. Tonight they'll see
a wool night, be rubbed with
its roughness. One man
thought a star had fallen
on the other side of camp.

Flame-waves pour near.
We lie down in midnight,
immerse, looking up through
an inch of warm creek that
upstream trout boiled in.
Water-fired, they bump by.
Our lungs swallow air hot
as coffee. One boy
sings a boy-song.
He wants up. He wants to
be with the impossible mother
of the flames. I remember his
lullaby, how his eyebrows
evaporated. He became
a configuration of steam.

Afterwards in the rummage
of the grub pile, some beans,
and bacon scorched topside.
No leavings of the burst sugar
or where the coffee discharged.
We flung some salt in each
other's eyes, to clean them,
then wept at what the fire
had not put out.

If you wake the coals
at night with your hoe,
if you scratch off
their burnt coats,
there is the skylight
into the earth, there in
the orange polish and
breathing.

      The squirrels will
not fly over it. The poor
will not chase dimes
down there. Boots smoke,
soles like boiling tacks.
You submerge to
your knees. Don't push
down on the glow.

A hand beginning to burn—
fingers an infusion of bees

arrive at your face—the hive
that isn't there.

Cautery of lightning
down the sap spines.
Roots ignite, untie from
the earth. Fever-bones
of the branches let
go of the sky. Arboreal

vertigo, closets of ash.
I push some over
with a glove. The bullyragged
pines drop into the ghost
duff. Almost a whoosh,
like someone jumping
off their roof into feathers.

Black feathers and then cement.

. . . .

I am
an outline in the ash.
Others sleep without moving,
nailed down by weariness.
Roots burn circuits beneath us.
My axe won't kill any more
shadows tonight. A fuse and wet
fingers touch in each of us.
I am too tired for water.
Tomorrow we'll find two sparrow
anatomies that did the fire-
dive off the powerlines,
fell to start this one.
They'll write the checks for next
month's bills. They'll feed
us. Their small decisions brought
us here, the coolest place
in the fire. A thunderhead
passes over, scattering us
in any direction. Mine—
a mercury drop swimming
around the palm of a hand.
No, a pearl
of rain slipping out of
the wind-tipped skillet
of a nasturtium leaf.

. . . .

Not one is going anywhere
except to inspect the transparent corners
for a way out. A purple shore crab
rises on sideways tiptoes
using a buddy as a stepladder
to push off into the impossible.
Its cruel reflection at the water top
and ascension of bubbles
keep sending hope to the downfallen.
Children have intimidated
the octopus all morning,
dirty hands in a saltwater grotto.
It has painted itself
white from the inside.
No one stops the woman
from dropping pennies
on its billowy head.
Stories say fishermen sometimes
turn one inside out
like a pillowcase.
In schoolroom aquaria
they often pull themselves
into the night leaking away
in the sound of janitor's keys.
They live less than five years
mate once
all hugs
then both die floating,
weak sacks pushed

by the wavery currents.
It wasn't suicide one night
when a Newport octopus
took its eyes
good as any human's
over the top of its circle of water,
translating the air with its arm,
its skin exit-sign green.
The slow arms' exodus began
wading out of the water
onto the floor. The following morning
they found it glued to the glass door
wound around the handles and limp.
All three hearts' compasses still set,
stuck on Yaquina Bay.

Their heads decay
from interior reasons,
become white bruises,
a way to finish their blue
six-foot bodies.
Pumped ocean
massages their gills.
Faces sigh and wilt.
Each one
could be my grandmother
whom we found
at Dammasch
in a rented bed,
nude and alone
near the end
of a sponge bath,
the washcloth
imprinted with a wet copy
of her hands,
the nurse gone
for the phone.
Are they trying
to say something
like a brain
when it's shaken out
of all its words,
lips making soft collisions,
drooping open frowns.
We do not comfort them
with our study,

our notetaking
calculating the inevitable.
Next visit they look
dipped in a silver bleach.
One lies on the tank floor,
a scallop-shaped fin
pointing up
like the last hand
of a drowning swimmer.
Others curl
in lazy alphabets,
SOS's
on a visible frequency.
We have come
to love the way
they rest together
side by side,
these long mutes
breathing in the same
puffed rhythms,
sharing the same water,
chins resting
on a rocky shelf.
We are near wolf eels,
patient shut-ins brought up
from dim fathoms
with too little decompression,
on display with a husband's wrath
wrapped like bull kelp around our necks,
and nowhere to go
but out.
Tonight, in a new state,
all of our old eels

replaced with cabezon sadness,
I watch you eat
dinner through the sliding patio door,
knowing I can push aside
the glass whenever I want,
and what pours
toward me is holdfast enough,
our version of grace
out of water.

Your lovely obsessions
calm these blue mornings
scuffed by the voices
of hungry jays.
What in sleep we remembered
crumbles like birdbell seeds
rain-loosened into mulberry shade.
Which are the animals
we adopt for ourselves today,
a blend of swimmers,
amblers and flyers?
From duckweed to palm trees,
to beyond and below,
we move and are moved.

At the zoo
each foot of these flamingos
collapses upward as it's raised
out of their pool,
black hooked bills
straining the water
in s-trails.
It is easy to imagine
feather-stitched bones,
the keeper's saw
that made their wings two-thirds
and independent of wind,
cries like a rusty stroller wheel.
They rest on top
of themselves

like a bright pillow,
two feet above the grass
on one locked knee,
with the other leg
stuck out to dry.
They seem to have
wire skeletons,
coat-hanger architecture
twisted into something
that balances.
Maybe they've fallen
off a carousel
and no one noticed.
I don't know.
It is here among
these logy acrobats
you say, "Marry me
if you know I'm dying.
For the benefits.
But not until then."
So like you.
Yet, we wander quiet
to the chimpanzee
shaking the storm
out of its cage,
spitting through the bars
at all the jeering adolescents,
until finally it gives
only a matted profile
and a look at fingers
too close to our own.

For the rest of the afternoon
I wonder about that time
when I'm supervisor
of your bone bits and ash,
would it be OK
if I put them
in with the elephants,
when they dust themselves
behind the ears
and under their bellies,
or toss sloppy bundles of timothy
onto the barren pastures
of their backs,
where you could ride
queen of things odd
and therefore beautiful above us all.

So much fog, how could we
measure it? It mutes the offshore
rocks that sketch the ocean
into tributaries, temporary water-
falls cleaning and feeding the cities
of stubborn mussels, the acres of barnacle
clutches a blundering hand could shred on.
We are out and walking, dewed already,
our shoes two-tone now, minutely heavier
with sand and a few weak leftover waves.
This fog began in our sleep
and continues, morning's gray
mirage we're always at the center of:
enclosure like night, but no fear.
We concentrate on the next step,
the next, on a gull testing its lonely
aerial sonar, bouncing its hunger
off our hearts, off the sanddollars'
moist snap under our wandering.
There is no way to retrace
what we've done, only a way into
the next step, into this brief cloud
we have always wanted, always wanted
to find each other and be lost in.

. . . .

A black lab mouths
the exhausted gull,
tugging and staring,
biting through its bones,
backing it out
to the tide's loose reach,
to the beginning of water,
transient imprint of a sand angel
gently scraped and left behind.
A thin inch of ocean
floats this transaction back
and forth, wings soaked,
too sore now, useless.
"Look, Joe," you say, "look at that."
And I say, "I know, Joe, I know."
Though neither of us is Joe,
something we have in common
besides this elegy performed
before father and son
who displace the mist
with the mist falling back in.
You unhook yourself
from hearing,
afraid of rusting
an expensive third ear,

warm now in your pocket.
I think it still listens:
taking in our silence,
the lowering hungry unseeable gulls,
and a few words I've been
wanting to say.

. . . .

Because he did not drink
the pineapple and methanol punch
(wood alcohol from the paint locker)
he was not the one who reversed
his insides onto the deck
of the merchantman. All they could
do was keep the blained unoccupied
sack of the man tied and blind,
then wrap him in a tarpaulin shroud.

When boredom chewed on them
and the homemade garlic salami
had run out (they'd hung it
above their bunks where it swayed
like the untensing cock of a horse)
they began robbing the lifeboats
one can at a time:
all of the beans, pound cakes,
great thumbs of raspberry jam.

Sailors returning safely to ancient Mikonos
built an island of churches
for the Aegean. One man kneeled
in a new religion each morning
and prayed for King Xerxes
of Persia, who, irritated
with the sea, whipped and
stabbed gashes in the waves
they called white horses.

. . . .

It is their fifth home
in more than two years,

two trout whose last
few eyefuls wore the laze

of an August lake stretched
by a loose, rock-warmed breeze.

They are beyond
the idea of a meal.

Besides to whom
would I serve this famous meat,

its flavor collapsed
in an ice-fog longer

than any Bitterroot winter.
They have lost their need

for seasons and lie
together heads to tails

soldered by a line
of blood and frost

without one heart
between them.

Below-the-waterline sailors
they hover near the bottom

of a memory now cryogenic.
I had not meant

to save them,
but found I could not

leave them melting
in a can of alley sun,

could not watch
that spectrum—a disintegration

begun by flies
scratching the envelope of ice

down to skin
and into smell.

At twenty I worked
three months in a zero-degree

warehouse stacking boxes of pies,
dinner-cut potatoes, Oregon raspberries

and glazed doughnuts in plastic two-packs.
I'd step from 7:30 A.M.

in the summer to a place
where it was February always,

with an intermittent artificial wind
from the freezer blower

keeping me
and all the food quiet.

On breaks a salesman would
sometimes pass one of my hands

under his smoky nostrils,
"Must have had a good time

last night. There's only
two things that smell like fish . . ."

I'd swallow the last
strength of my coffee,

my nose thawed and leaking,
and open the door

to visit the cold again,
where I'd curse his half-moon belly

and the air-conditioned Oldsmobile
he drove too fast.

The salesman probably ate
too much of his livelihood

and choked on more and more.
I give one trout to him.

The other is for the man
who tugged it out of the lake

that day, dug it empty
with his fat thumb,

who several weeks later
found out what the fish learned.

All I know is the day
after he died a dog

from a downslope ranch
strayed on my cabin porch

and circled its mouth
for an hour

around something irreplaceable,
a sound that cleaned

the afternoon of words,
then left trotting

away through the snow,
hushed for a way to keep warm.

In memoriam Richard Hugo

. . . .

Most of their feathers are dead,
except where they begin, inside,
already dying. So all flights become round-

trips like the avenues and cul-de-sacs
blood finds, until it relaxes,
in the private positions

we finally stop in.
I know of gulls thrown out
of storms, but no mourning

dove has ever given up
on my porch, no crow
in the garden tomatoes,

nor finch in midair.
Field guides explain color,
vagrant range,

the vague translations of a song,
but nothing of the distance
that develops into absence.

Let's say they fall upward:
sparrow with an unlucky heart,
broken wrist of the mallard's wing,

and all the others,
until they find the highest wind,
where they circle the earth

in a frozen migration,
sometimes scraping
the quiet ceiling of the world.

· ·

This blue, these floating things
uncovered and different each morning, each memory,
beach- and rock-startled fragments,
pieces of pieces roughly washed,
obedient tumblers uplifted and scattered
on a repose of sand, the ever-fetching water.

Our ambling attentions guide us to water.
Among this salty debris, plain things,
cold former homes of the scattered,
acorns of shells, hardened meat of their bodies' memory
recalled in whorls. Sun-washed
bits of neptune, shattered whelks, false angel wing fragments . . .

We've subdued our ex-lives into fragments.
Water was our rescuer, afternoons of water,
a car blanket, creek stones washed
by uncertain eddies, things
our eyes would follow like swirls of memory,
here and there the anxiety appeared and scattered.

Your husband and you, me, all scattered,
all scared, diminished, fragments,
the sky dropping to earth, memory
of your wedding ring tugged off, the water
in the kitchen sink overflowing, things
like tears, faces made by them, unevenly washed.

Those sufferings begin their dusk, and the washed
ashore don't mind being scattered
about with their gritty hearts of sand, the things
they've become, to be selected as fragments,
warmed by a hand pinked by water,
something for a pocket, irregular shapes of memory.

Drift bottles of memory.
Sea palms dead, tousled and washed
next to our footprints dissolving. Water
takes what it wants eventually, the scattered
become more scattered, fragments
of all our water days become those things

we water our dreams with, becoming scattered
during our waking, memory in fragments
washed over us, the blue dried, all our floating things.

OVERLOOKING THE PACIFIC, FAMILY REUNION, CELEBRATING MY BROTHER'S CHILD, ECOLA STATE PARK

This is the gray that fills
in green, that loads up on drizzle,
       overflows into sword ferns,
       retreats into mosses.

The world below our knees
wades in it. Shoes squelch
       with puddles inside.
       We've come to eat

in the mist, to stand around
a salt-air picnic,
       wet napkins and holiday spoons.
       Storytelling inside a cloud.

No fire. No one chewing
aluminum hot dogs. A fat
       damp Sunday celebrating
       the first new Pavlich

in thirty years. He craps and cries
and wonders what we are.
       We fog ourselves
       with beer washed brisk

in the creek. I hope a heron
lives here. It must have its own
            definition of weekend:
            dogs, fishing line to trip over

(ankle-slicer), softball in the weeds,
a drowned watermelon hugged by stones.
            I learned a phobia
            at the crumbly cliff.

A warning sign had to be moved
east often. Every few years
            less and less
            to stand on.

I imagined falling with a meadow,
gulls hanging above me then ruffling off,
            some kinnikinnick in my hand.
            The more I fell the farther

I'd have to fall, until I broke
on the backs of rockfish,
            to be born again as a crab
            needling and feeling

my way through unlit
deep saline rooms of hell,
            my glasses, alone, reading
            through the intestines of an angel shark.

Another beer. Baked beans cold
in their sludge. My father now
          a grandfather drifts some
          of his face to the other side.

It's our new joke: an old man
in an impression of an old man
          after a stroke.
          Little whispered ghosts

spit out of his mouth. Left arm
displaced like a storm-hung door.
          Hinges. Screws missing.
          The anchor of his mind

thrown overboard. He and I now laughing
pink. The baby grabs for the joker's
          nose, a thumb lost
          in his nostril.

Just rehearsing, my father says,
could happen tomorrow. We unchuckle
          over pie. The ocean
          lightens into a white shine,

the horizon polished, clouds a silent
movie heaven. I want to see
          if my nude nephew floats.
          Hold him over

the surf. He is already wave-haunted,
voyeur of all this watery wear and tear.
        For a few minutes we face
        where we will never go.

Let the tides inside him wander
and find their way.
        Let him know the sound
        of the daughters and sons

recycled inside me: their voices the last note
of the mourning dove. I have let them
        loose like unhooked buoys
        drifting beyond the swells.

This is not mourning. I will
show him what I can:
        driftwood refined, returning
        to shore. The fires made

of them, the ocean emerging
as sweat, moistening the flames.
        Homeless kelp in piles
        slipping around each other,

they have nothing else to hold.
An opal worm rich in its glisten.
        I will show him what might
        be there and then I'll give him back.

The days of gliding, of running
upearth, wild spark pain-points
flaring inside my thighs,
brads tapped into calves
by the hammers of endurance,

are gone.

My feet step on a repeating
series of ampersands, forty
minutes long,

stutter of knee-pops circling
a neighborhood gone to jobs,
past a crewcut wrestling
sheetrock, wondering why-the-hell
I'm not working.

But this is my employment,
lugging around a glass of beer
from every bar in Missoula,

burning up oily smoke
through the stitch-holes of my pores,

climbing up out of the ass of depression.

Today into the wind like running
through the shallow end of a pool,

inhaling white gnats,

each breath with its own comma following it,
the pavement smarting exclamations,

my ears headphoned with sung black Christ
according to the Spirit of Memphis Quartet,

the five of us are "Walking with Jesus,"

God tight in the laces of my shoes,
in the pants the gray of which

I grew up on. (If I still listened to
my childhood religion, I'd be jogging on my knees.)

Joy all over
me like sweat, my belly

bouncing in the rhythm
like a cycloptic breast,

like the moon with a loose
vertical hold.
                    On the final loop

around the water project
it's a doo-wopped "I'm coming up Lord,
                      I'm coming up soon . . ."

Julius Cheeks leading the Sensational

Nightingales and leading me around
the plugs of dogshit and construction
nails, the finches riding the purple

crowns of star thistles,

near enough to the unseen egret
who rises up in stiff arced circles
the color of surrender.

The Iowa Poetry Prize Winners

1987
Elton Glaser, *Tropical Depressions*
Michael Pettit, *Cardinal Points*

1988
Mary Ruefle, *The Adamant*
Bill Knott, *Outremer*

1989
Terese Svoboda, *Laughing Africa*
Conrad Hilberry, *Sorting the Smoke*

The Edwin Ford Piper
Poetry Award Winners

1990
Lynda Hull, *Star Ledger*
Philip Dacey, *Night Shift at the Crucifix Factory*

1991
Walter Pavlich, *Running near the End of the World*
Greg Pape, *Sunflower Facing the Sun*